SAM
HOUSTON

TEXAS HERO

SPECIAL LIVES IN HISTORY THAT BECOME

Signature LIVES

SAM
HOUSTON
TEXAS HERO

by Susan R. Gregson

Content Adviser: Walter M. Woodward,
Curator of Collections, Sam Houston Memorial Museum,
Huntsville, Texas

Reading Adviser: Rosemary G. Palmer, Ph.D.,
Department of Literacy, College of Education,
Boise State University

COMPASS POINT BOOKS MINNEAPOLIS, MINNESOTA

Compass Point Books
3109 West 50th Street, #115
Minneapolis, MN 55410

Visit Compass Point Books on the Internet at *www.compasspointbooks.com*
or e-mail your request to *custserv@compasspointbooks.com*

Editor: Editorial Directions, Inc.
Lead Designer: Jaime Martens
Page Production: Noumenon Creative
Photo Researcher: Marcie C. Spence
Cartographer: XNR Productions, Inc.
Educational Consultant: Diane Smolinski

Managing Editor: Catherine Neitge
Creative Director: Keith Griffin
Editorial Director: Carol Jones

Library of Congress Cataloging-in-Publication Data
Gregson, Susan R.
 Sam Houston : Texas hero / by Susan R. Gregson.
  p. cm. – (Signature lives)
 Includes bibliographical references and index.
 ISBN 0-7565-1004-X (hard cover)
 1. Houston, Sam, 1793-1863—Juvenile literature. 2. United States.
Congress. Senate—Biography—Juvenile literature. 3. Governors—
Texas—Biography—Juvenile literature. 4. Legislators—United States—
Biography—Juvenile literature. 5. Texas—History—To 1846—
Juvenile literature. I. Title. II. Series.
 F390.H84G744 2006
 976.4'04'092–dc22   2005009098

AMERICAN FRONTIER ERA

By the late 1700s, the United States was growing into a nation of homesteaders, politicians, mountain men, and American dreams. Manifest Destiny propelled settlers to push west, conquering and "civilizing" from coast to coast. In keeping with this vision, world leaders hammered out historic agreements such as the Louisiana Purchase, which drastically increased U.S. territory. This ambition often led to bitter conflicts with Native Americans trying to protect their way of life and their traditional lands. Life on the frontier was often filled with danger and difficulties. The people who wove their way into American history overcame these challenges with a courage and conviction that defined an era and shaped a nation.

Table of Contents

Chapter

1 OLD SAM JACINTO

❧✦❧

Sam Houston and his men were tired, hungry, and more than a little grumpy. They had been marching and riding along Texas wagon roads for days. Houston would have said they were marching bravely into history. Many of his men would have said that they weren't marching, they were running like a bunch of chickens. How had it come to this?

In 1834, Texas was part of a Mexican state. Settlers came from Europe and the American East and South to make new lives in Mexico's Texas, a vast land of rolling plains that seemed to stretch on forever. The Mexican government, uncomfortable with the growing Texan population, restricted the settlers' rights.

Many Texans and even some Mexican Texans, or

Presidio de La Bahia was built by the Spanish near Goliad, Texas, in 1749.

Tejanos, wanted Texas to be an independent state within Mexico. Other people wanted Texas to become completely independent of Mexico. That year, the Mexican army rolled into Texas intent on occupying towns and disarming citizens. Independence-seekers and the Mexican army began to skirmish. Texas was on the verge of a bloody revolution.

On March 2, 1836, representatives from different areas of Texas formally declared their independence from Mexico. Cold spring weather didn't stop the council of men from gathering in a shop still under

In 1830, Mexico controlled the southwestern part of North America.

construction to draft and sign a constitution for the new Republic of Texas. They set up a temporary government and confirmed Sam Houston as the commander in chief of the army.

Houston's army was a ragtag group of experienced militia and volunteer civilians. The men—from Virginia, Tennessee, Louisiana, Kentucky, Alabama, and other places—were willing to fight for their adopted home. Unfortunately, the bold character that made the men good pioneers also made them difficult to organize. Some of them didn't even have guns and ammunition.

While Houston and the other leaders signed the new Texas Constitution, Mexican leader Antonio Lopez de Santa Anna and his troops stormed a fort in San Antonio known as the Alamo. The Mexican army killed all of the defenders at the Alamo, stacked their bodies like firewood, and burned them. Santa Anna, who called himself the Napoleon of the West, warned the citizens of Texas that he would not tolerate revolution.

About three weeks later, Colonel James W. Fannin and about 400 men surrendered to Santa Anna's general, José de Urrea, at La Bahia fort in the town of Goliad. The Texans and

The Republic of Texas shared its birthday, March 2, with Sam Houston, an eloquent, commanding man who had made Texas his home only a few years earlier.

Antonio Lopez de Santa Anna was born on February 21, 1794, in Jalapa, Mexico. He led the Mexican army in the fight against independence for Texas.

their commander expected to be treated as prisoners of war. Instead, Santa Anna ordered their execution. By this time, terrified Texans were leaving all their possessions behind and fleeing their homes to escape the Mexican army.

Houston gathered his troops and retreated east toward Louisiana. He was secretive about his plans. His men wanted to attack, but Houston insisted on waiting. When the time was right, he led his men to a stunning victory against Santa

Anna at San Jacinto. Some of his men would write later that their general was a coward for not going right into battle. More would stand by his actions. Regardless of that debate, most historians rank the victory at San Jacinto as one of the most decisive battles in world history—and it marked the beginning of independence for Texas.

Sam Houston is the only person to have ever been the governor of two U.S. states: Tennessee (1827–1829) and Texas (1859–1861).

Sam Houston—nicknamed Old Sam Jacinto by the men who fought with him—was 43 years old at that famous battle. He had already been an Indian agent, a congressman, and a governor. He was lured to Texas by its vast expanse; it seemed just big enough to hold his big dreams. While U.S. statehood would have to wait because of the issue of slavery, the larger-than-life Houston went on to shape Texas' destiny. ✑

2 RUNAWAY BOY

Chapter

ꙮ

Sam Houston was born in Virginia in 1793. George Washington was president of the new United States. It was nearly two decades after the Revolutionary War. Life in the eastern states was settling into a routine—one that young Sam quickly found boring as the nation entered the 1800s. It seemed to him that all the excitement was farther west, where pioneers were pushing the boundaries of new settlement into the wild frontier.

Anywhere else had to be more exciting. Sam lived on a farm with his parents, four older brothers, one younger brother, and three younger sisters. Restless, impatient, and bright, Sam didn't care much for sitting in a classroom. He was a voracious reader, though, and would often lie on

A settler leads his sheep back to his homestead in Tennessee, the state where Houston spent much of his youth.

the floor near his father's books, reading for hours. He especially liked the books about heroes and epic battles.

When he wasn't reading, Sam whittled wood. He would whittle throughout his life. As a grownup, he used his whittling time to think things through or to make tiny carved figures that he liked to give to people.

When Sam was 13, his father, Samuel, died unexpectedly. The family sold their farm, and Sam's mother, Elizabeth, gathered her children and headed to Tennessee. They purchased more than 400 acres (160 hectares) of land there and began building a new home.

At first, Tennessee seemed exciting. The Houstons lived in a blockhouse with other families while their farmhouse was being built. The blockhouse was a group of homes clustered together to protect families from attacks by hostile Indian tribes. As exciting as it appeared to Sam, the last Indian attack in the area had taken place more than 10 years earlier.

It wasn't long before the Houston clan settled into their farmhouse. With the new farm came chores. Sam's older brothers kept dragging him away from his daydreams and books and forcing him to help plant and plow the fields. Soon, however, he was dodging his brothers. Figuring that he

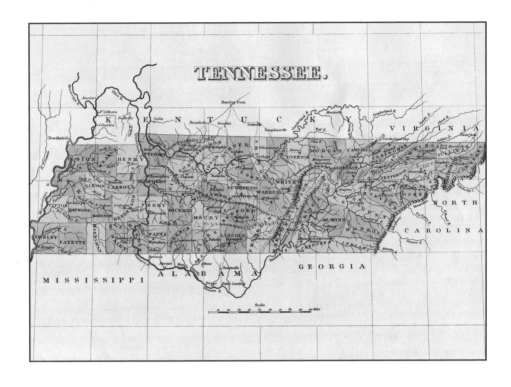

TENNESSEE.

An 1826 map of Tennessee

just didn't like working the farm, his brothers sent him to a nearby town to work in a general store partly owned by their mother. Measuring flour and weighing potatoes for customers was not as exciting as reading books about heroes and dreaming of glory, though, and Sam ran away.

Lugging as many of his favorite books as he could carry, Sam headed west to an island in the Tennessee River. The island was home to a band of Cherokee. The 16-year-old boy found their lives much more interesting than farming and clerking in a store. The Cherokee chief, Oolooteka, also called

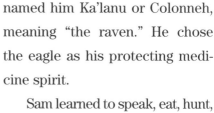

The words frontier and wilderness make people think of danger, hardship, wild animals, and few luxuries. In the early 1800s, however, there were few differences between living in a city and living on the frontier. While there were fewer neighbors on the frontier and a greater risk of attack from Indians, neither location had running water, electricity, garbage disposal, sewer systems, or good medical care.

John Jolly, adopted Sam and named him Ka'lanu or Colonneh, meaning "the raven." He chose the eagle as his protecting medicine spirit.

Sam learned to speak, eat, hunt, and dress like his new Cherokee family. He even learned to dance, something he loved for the rest of his life. Sam probably played a popular ball game, similar to today's lacrosse. After a time, his brothers tracked him down and insisted that he return to the farm. Sam later recalled that he told them, "I preferred measuring deer tracks to tape, and that I liked the wild liberty of the Red men better than the tyranny of my own brothers. I told them to go home and leave me in peace." Eventually, his exasperated brothers left him alone.

Over the next three years, Houston sometimes went back to the farm to see how things were going and borrow money from his mother. But it wasn't long before he was back on the island with Oolooteka. He just didn't have the patience for the routine of his old life. During the three years Sam

Houston lived with the Cherokee, he came to understand their customs and way of life. Later, as a government official, he would use his understanding of the Cherokee to deal fairly and effectively with other tribes.

Some people say that Houston began drinking around this time. Buying alcohol was expensive, and he soon found himself $100 in debt. That was a lot of money in the early 1800s. Houston knew he needed to pay back the money and that would mean leaving the Cherokee for good and getting a job.

As a young man, Sam Houston preferred the life of the Cherokee to farming.

Houston opened a school in Maryville, Tennessee. He wore his long hair tied down his back. His students paid their tuition in cash, corn, and fabric, which he used to make his shirts. At more than 6 feet (183 centimeters) tall, he often strode through the classroom with a stick in his hand. He must have appeared imposing to his students. After just one term, Houston had enough money to repay his debt, and that was the end of his brief teaching career. He wanted to do bigger and bolder things.

It was 1813, and the United States was fighting the War of 1812. England had been stirring up western tribes against American settlers and overtaking American ships at sea. Americans resented England's meddling in U.S. business and its attempt to gain control of the western part of North America.

U.S. Army recruiters arrived in Maryville in March 1813 with flags flying. Stirred by an Army sergeant's patriotic speech and the desire to go where the action was, Houston enlisted as a soldier. The war seemed like the perfect opportunity to become a hero.

Before Houston went off to war, his mother gave him a thin gold ring with the word *honor* engraved on it. He wore the ring until years later when his wife slipped it off his finger after his death. His mother sent him off telling him, "While the door of my

Sam Houston was such a commanding presence that people who met him described him as being anywhere from 6 feet 3 inches (190 cm) to 6 feet 6 inches (198 cm) tall. His military records and passport say he was 6 feet 2 inches (188 cm), but his family thinks he may have grown a little after he entered the military. He probably seemed taller because people described him as being "straight as an arrow" and of "magnificent form" and "fine contour." One of Houston's descendants used a set of crutches to guess that he was just under 6 feet 3 inches (190 cm) tall.

cottage is always open to brave men, it is eternally shut against cowards." Sam had no intention of being a coward. ✑

The USS Constitution was victorious in a battle against the British in 1812.

3 SOLDIER AND STATESMAN

❧❦❧

Sam Houston proved to be an excellent soldier and moved quickly up in rank. His bravery wasn't tested, though, until March 1814 in Alabama. Houston was part of General Andrew Jackson's Army and in charge of a company of soldiers. They were facing off against a tribe of Creek called the Red Sticks. The Army and the Red Sticks were face-to-face across an earth and log barricade at a place called Horseshoe Bend. The first person to scramble over the barricade was immediately killed. Houston was the second person to go over as he led his company into dozens of small battles.

Many soldiers died just getting over the barricade. Houston was shot in the groin with a barbed arrow. A soldier tried but could not pull out the

Sam Houston enlisted in the U.S. Army in 1813 and became an accomplished soldier.

Chief Red Eagle and his Creek followers who supported the Shawnee warrior Tecumseh were called Red Sticks. While many of his followers were killed at the Battle of Horseshoe Bend, Red Eagle—whose name was William Weatherford, the son of a Scottish trader and a Creek mother—was not at the bloody battle. Still wanted as the Red Stick leader, the chief would later surrender to Andrew Jackson in return for getting safe passage for Red Stick women and children taken prisoner at the battle. Red Eagle was also able to keep his farm in Alabama, where he eventually returned to live.

arrow and told Houston to find a medic. Sam Houston pointed his sword at the soldier and demanded he yank out the arrow. The soldier tore it out and left a gaping wound that would never heal. A doctor stopped to dress the wound, and General Jackson, who commended Houston, told him to rest.

Houston didn't want to rest and headed back into the fight. The battle was going well for the U.S. Army, but there was one fortress where the Red Sticks fired rifles from tiny holes. The persistent Houston led his men once again into the heat of battle and was shot twice in the shoulder and once in the arm. He collapsed, his men halted, and Jackson eventually set the fortress ablaze with flaming arrows. The Battle of Horseshoe Bend was over. More than 900 Indians were dead. The British would receive no more help from the Creek as they battled the United States in the War of 1812.

Houston was left on the battlefield with the dead and
dying. Soldiers said he
wouldn't last the night.
When they found him
alive the next morn-
ing, they placed him
on a litter and dragged
him 60 miles (96 kilo-
meters) to a fort. He still
seemed so near death
that the soldiers left him at
the fort in the middle of the
wilderness. Houston survived and
was eventually taken to a doctor in New
Orleans who was able to remove the last bullet from
his shoulder. But Houston did not regain enough
strength to return to battle before the war ended.

Creek warrior chief Menawa was one of the few Native Americans to survive the Battle of Horseshoe Bend.

Although he had been badly injured, Lieutenant
Sam Houston still planned to make the military
his career. His next assignment was to help the government persuade the Cherokee to move to
Arkansas Territory. The Cherokee welcomed their
old friend and agreed with him that settlers would
not let the Indians live among them. Houston told
them that Tennessee was becoming crowded and
they should move west. Chief Oolooteka and his
people agreed to move.

John C. Calhoun of South Carolina served the United States as a congressman, secretary of war, senator, secretary of state, and vice president. He was an ardent supporter of states' rights and slavery.

Ten years earlier, however, Chief Oolooteka's older brother, Chief Tahlhontusky, had gone west when the U.S. government promised his band some money if they moved off their land. They had never received the money. Chief Tahlhontusky had returned to Tennessee. He told the governor that he wanted to go to Washington, D.C., and talk to the secretary of war about this broken promise. The governor asked Houston to go with the Cherokee to Washington. To make them feel more comfortable about visiting U.S. government officials, Houston dressed like the Cherokee. He wore buckskins with a blanket around his shoulders and a silk turban around his head.

When the group arrived in Washington, D.C., Secretary of War John C. Calhoun made more promises and said he would talk to the Cherokee later. He sent them from his office and asked Houston to stay behind. Calhoun angrily asked Houston why he came to his office dressed like an Indian. Houston didn't think he needed to explain his actions to an arrogant man who did not understand that he had done it for

General Andrew Jackson (1767–1845) would become the nation's seventh president.

diplomacy. He left Calhoun's office without apologizing and decided he didn't much like the man. The feeling was mutual.

Houston decided he couldn't stay in an army led by men like Calhoun, so he resigned. He kept in touch with General Jackson, however, and visited

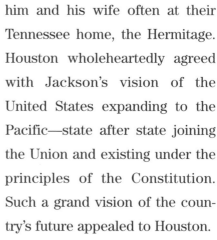

Sam Houston often talked about himself in the third person. Instead of saying "I was born," he would say "Houston was born." He picked up this habit from the Cherokee, who traditionally speak in the third person.

him and his wife often at their Tennessee home, the Hermitage. Houston wholeheartedly agreed with Jackson's vision of the United States expanding to the Pacific—state after state joining the Union and existing under the principles of the Constitution. Such a grand vision of the country's future appealed to Houston.

Grand visions didn't pay the bills, though, and Houston needed a career. He began studying law and became a lawyer after just six months, instead of the typical 18 months of study. While studying law at that quick pace, he also made time to act in local drama productions. He could easily make people laugh, and he loved dressing for the parts. This flair for the dramatic served him well throughout his life, as he mesmerized people with his booming speeches and fancy clothes for every special occasion.

Houston opened a law office near Nashville, Tennessee, and dressed the part of the new professional in bright coats and a beaver hat. Handsome, tall, and outgoing, it wasn't long before he entered a political race and was elected to office. In 1823, he became one of Tennessee's congressmen.

The first thing he did after being elected was to

The Hermitage was the home of Andrew Jackson.

buy another hat. The second was to vow to find a way to get back at Calhoun. Before he could do that, however, he had to learn to get along in Washington, D.C. That wasn't always easy.

In an argument over who would be the best postmaster for Nashville, Houston disagreed with Secretary of State Henry Clay. He made some negative remarks about the man Clay wanted for the office. When the man heard what Houston had said, he challenged him to a duel. In the early 1800s, it was common for men to duel to defend their honor or the honor of a loved one.

Houston was reluctant to duel, but finally gave in to the challenge. His old friend and mentor, Andrew Jackson, was an expert duelist and gave Houston some pointers. Houston shot the man, badly wounding him, and then fretted about it.

Fortunately, the duel did not make Houston any less popular, and in 1827, he campaigned for governor of Tennessee. Campaigning for office always energized Houston. He enjoyed speaking to crowds and winning them over to his point of view. He loved making dashing appearances on stately stallions at the polls. One observer described Houston as:

> *dressed in a bell-crowned beaver hat, standing collar, military stock, ruffled shirt, black satin vest, and black trousers gathered at the waist with legs the same size from seat to ankle. A gorgeous Indian hunting shirt, encircled by a beaded red sash with polished metal clasp was thrown over his broad shoulders in place of a coat. His pumps sported silver buckles and his silk socks were lavishly embroidered.*

Houston's commanding presence helped him easily win the governorship. When Andrew Jackson was elected president of the United States in 1828, many people considered Houston a possible successor to Jackson.

Having experienced political success, the 35-year-old Houston wanted to round out the personal side of his life. He met and married a young woman named Eliza Allen in 1829. She was the 18-year-old daughter of an old friend.

Houston was head over heels in love with Eliza, but she may have felt pressured into the marriage by her family. The two were married only three months when Eliza returned to her parents' home. Rumors about why she left Houston quickly swirled around Tennessee society.

Eliza's family hinted that Houston was a domineering, jealous man who drank too much. The newspapers of the day gleefully publicized the scandal. Houston's friends begged him to set the record straight, but Houston refused to say anything bad about Eliza in order to defend himself. Soon the ugly rumors drove him to resign as governor. To escape this stunning turn of events, Houston did what he had done so long ago—he ran away to his Cherokee family. ✍

Houston liked to tell the story of a boy who got the best of him. While fishing in Illinois, his line became entangled with the line of a boy who was fishing nearby. Houston asked the young fisher to move, and the boy told him, "You blasted old shortcoat, go elsewhere yourself and fish." When Houston scolded the boy for his disrespect, the boy shouted that he knew Houston was really a horse thief named Sam Dawson. "Now you're putting on a big shine and calling yourself Sam Houston," the boy said angrily before grabbing Houston's fishing pole and tossing it into the river. Houston said that even men in Congress had never left him so speechless.

4 FROM WANDERER TO TEXAN

෴

Houston left his home and traveled aimlessly by foot and steamboat. Wanting anonymity, he introduced himself as Samuels. He drank a lot and tried to forget his humiliation in Tennessee. At one point, the only thing that kept him from jumping from a steamboat was the sight of an eagle, his medicine spirit, swooping overhead and soaring west.

Longing for his Cherokee friends, Houston headed to Arkansas Territory, near present-day Oklahoma, and found Chief Oolooteka. Though years had passed, the chief welcomed his adopted son again. Houston wasted no time settling into Cherokee ways. He dressed in a doeskin shirt and leather leggings, wore his hair tied in the back, and covered his shoulders with bright blankets. He

After his wife, Eliza, left him, Sam Houston went back to live with the Cherokee.

promised never to speak English again and even promised to unite all the western tribes.

Houston traveled all over the West, visiting countless tribes and working as an Indian agent, someone who promoted the interests of the tribes to the federal government. Back East, even President Jackson wondered why Houston was trying so hard to unite the tribes. He was concerned that Houston might have plans to conquer Mexico and rule the West, but Houston assured Jackson he would never do anything like that against his country.

When he wasn't working, he was drinking, and some of the Cherokee nicknamed him the Big Drunk. Drinking seemed to be the only way he could blot out the vicious things people had said about him in Tennessee. In a Cherokee ceremony in 1830, he married Oolooteka's niece, Diana Rogers, who is often called Tiana by historians. They ran a trading post out of their house and entertained visitors. Houston even ran for Cherokee council but was defeated. Depressed, he kept drinking.

The Cherokee people call themselves aniyvwiya, or "the real people." Besides the directions of north, south, east, and west, Cherokee traditionally recognize three other directions. They are: above (up), below (down), and center (where you are).

In autumn of 1831, word came to Houston that his mother was seriously ill. He traveled to

Tennessee to be with her when she died. In December, he traveled to Washington, D.C., with a delegation of Cherokee and was swept up in the middle of controversy again.

Ohio Representative William Stanbery accused Houston of being corrupt. He did it as part of the official Congressional Record, on the floor of the House chamber. When he heard about it, Houston became livid. He sent Stanbery a note challenging him to a duel. Stanbery ignored Houston but started carrying pistols. He stayed out of Houston's way, until one evening, when Houston saw him walking on Pennsylvania Avenue and rushed to confront him.

The Cherokee, like many Indian tribes, believed that some animals were the living forms of spirits that could protect humans. They called these medicine spirits. Houston chose the eagle as his medicine spirit.

Houston called Stanbery a rascal and whacked him again and again with his cane. He jumped on the congressman's back and toppled him. Stanbery tried to shoot Houston, but his pistol misfired. Houston continued to punch Stanbery until two friends pulled him away.

Battered and bruised, Stanbery persuaded the House of Representatives to arrest Houston. The next day, Stanbery wrote, "I was waylaid in the street by the giant Tennessean, knocked down by a bludgeon, and badly wounded, all for words spoken in my place in the House of Representatives."

Francis Scott Key's "The Star-Spangled Banner" became the official U.S. national anthem in 1931.

Andrew Jackson didn't want his old friend humiliated by the House. It would be bad for Jackson's reputation as well as Houston's. He told Houston to get out of his Cherokee clothing and gave him some money for a suit. Francis Scott Key, author of "The Star-Spangled Banner," was Houston's lawyer, but he wasn't doing a great job. When Key became sick, Houston took over his own defense and, in his new clothes, impressed the

House with a series of thundering speeches about freedom and democracy.

The House mildly reprimanded Houston, and a weight seemed to lift from his shoulders. He spent several months in Washington, visiting with President Jackson and catching up on politics. Jackson then sent Houston to Texas as a diplomat to work with Indian tribes.

The Stanbery ordeal had been good medicine for Houston. He returned to the Cherokee just long enough to give his house and possessions to Diana. Then he rode to Texas where settlers were getting ready to petition the Mexican government to make Texas an independent state.

Houston traveled across Texas and spoke with people about the situation there. He reported what he found out to Jackson, who was very interested in what was going on in Texas. The United States wanted to buy Texas from Mexico but had been turned down. Both Jackson and Houston thought Texas would be a good addition to the United States.

Back in Washington, Jackson was struggling with Houston's old nemesis, John Calhoun, who was advocating a nullification doctrine for South Carolina. This meant that if a state didn't like a law passed by the federal government, it didn't have to obey the law. The nullification doctrine also said that if the federal government tried to use force to get its way, a state had the right to separate from the national government. President Jackson was stunned and furious. Publicly, he said that those who supported nullification were acting as if the United States were not a nation. Behind closed doors, Jackson promised to hang anyone who defied federal laws.

The United States remained divided even after Calhoun stopped talking about nullification. The biggest division was over slavery. This issue came up each time a state was admitted to the Union. Would the state be a free state or a slave state? Neither side wanted the other to have more power. Jackson began to think that statehood for Texas would have to wait, even if Texans figured out a way

Philadelphia, Pennsylvania, served as the capital of the United States until October 1800 when Washington, D.C., became the new capital.

to become independent from Mexico.

People in Texas were divided over whether to work peacefully with Mexico or fight for independence. The Mexican government intended to enforce its constitutional ban on slavery, but many Anglo Texans supported slavery. The Mexican government also opened a chain of military posts, tightened trade with the United States, and closed Texas' borders to immigrants from the United States.

Some people hoped for a peaceful resolution of these issues when the Mexican leadership changed in 1833, and soldier and politician Santa Anna became the new president of Mexico. Texans thought Santa Anna might be more receptive to the idea of Mexican statehood for Texas. They were wrong.

> *Houston sometimes signed his name "Paul Sam Houston" on documents until the mid-1830s. His son Andrew Jackson Houston told a researcher that the Mexican government required settlers to convert to the Roman Catholic religion and take the name of a saint as a first name. Houston chose the first name Paul when he was baptized. The Mexican government required people to sign all court papers with the full baptismal name.*

5 FIGHTING FOR INDEPENDENCE

❧❦❧

When Santa Anna became president, he abolished Mexico's constitutional government. He raised taxes on Anglos and reaffirmed Mexico's ban on slavery, which angered the majority of Anglo Texans, who were pro-slavery. In April 1833, Texas leader Stephen F. Austin traveled to Mexico to meet with Santa Anna. He hoped to peacefully discuss the Texans' desire to establish themselves as an independent state. Instead, Santa Anna imprisoned him for the crime of stirring up revolt in Texas.

Santa Anna wasted no time sending Mexican troops into Texas. At first, Texans stood up to the Mexican army and won a handful of small battles. Leaders of the movement for Texas independence formed a provisional government, and in November

Stephen F. Austin led the first English-speaking settlers into Texas in 1822 and established a colony on the Brazos River.

1835, that government appointed Houston a major general in the Texas army.

In December, 300 Texans in San Antonio moved through the city in hand-to-hand combat against the Mexican troops stationed there. The battle lasted five days, and in the end 1,000 Mexicans surrendered. The Texans sent Mexican leader General Martin Perfecto de Cos back to his brother-in-law, Santa Anna, with a warning to stay out of Texas.

Houston cautioned anyone who would listen that though they won the battle, Santa Anna would never give up without a bigger fight. He realized that the Texans had won these first victories in spite of the fact that the Texas army was not well trained or well organized. Houston worried that the bold men pouring into Texas and joining the army were not the kind of people who liked to take direction. It took a very independent person to settle a new land, and Texas was full of strong people with their own opinions.

General Houston met with Colonel James Fannin in Goliad, Texas. The general was worried about what he saw. Fannin was not a decisive leader, and the more than 400 men under him were undisciplined and had no direction. Most of the rest of the Texas army was spread out in small groups under the command of six colonels,

This Mexican newspaper contains an article in which Santa Anna denounces the Mexican defeat in San Antonio and calls for Mexicans to avenge the honor of their country and punish the Texans.

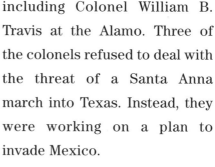

> Antonio Lopez de
> Santa Anna served as
> president of Mexico 11
> different times. From
> the end of Spanish rule
> in 1821 through 1847,
> Mexico's government
> was very unstable. By
> 1854, half of Mexico
> had become part of the
> United States and
> eventually became all
> or part of Arizona,
> California, Colorado,
> Nevada, New
> Mexico, Texas, Utah,
> and Wyoming.

including Colonel William B. Travis at the Alamo. Three of the colonels refused to deal with the threat of a Santa Anna march into Texas. Instead, they were working on a plan to invade Mexico.

Houston was able to persuade Fannin not to go along with the plan to invade Mexico. He told Fannin that the ranks must regroup, prepare, and drill. Houston believed that it would be better to take the time to prepare than to rush off to battle.

Eventually, word came that Santa Anna was headed to Texas with 7,000 men to squash the Texas revolt and take back San Antonio. Houston ordered Travis to abandon the Alamo and burn it to keep it out of Santa Anna's hands, but Travis and his men refused to leave.

Houston traveled throughout eastern Texas to make sure the Cherokee and other tribes there would not support Mexico in a war. He met with an old friend, Chief Bowles, who assured him the Cherokee would support Texas.

On February 23, 1836, Santa Anna arrived in San Antonio with more than 1,000 men. They were met by the band of Texas rebels behind the walls of the Alamo. Travis led the military, and frontiersman Jim Bowie led the volunteer army. American wilderness hero Davy Crockett fought at the Alamo, too.

The Mexican army flew a red banner and played a song signaling that Santa Anna would draw no quarter, a military term meaning the Mexican army would have no mercy and take no prisoners. Travis and his men fired cannons in response. Santa Anna ordered his men to attack the fort. His army fired on the Alamo for 13 days.

James Bowie was a famous frontiersman who went to Texas in about 1828. He became a colonel in the Texas army and served at the Alamo.

Travis busily wrote letters describing the situation at the Alamo and asking for help. He sent messengers to deliver them. In one letter he asked Fannin to join him at the Alamo. Fannin was in no hurry to join Travis and get involved in the fight. When he finally did get his men under way, the oxen didn't want to move and wagons broke down. Fannin gave up and never made it to San Antonio.

Travis also sent several pleas to towns around San Antonio and to the government. He pleaded for more weapons and ammunition. About 35 men arrived from Gonzales, Texas. In one famous letter addressed to the people of Texas and all Americans, the colonel wrote, "I will never surrender or retreat. Victory or Death." More help would never arrive.

On March 1, a group of 59 men, including Houston, gathered at Washington-on-the-Brazos to write a declaration of Texas' independence and a constitution for the newly declared republic. The day before, messengers had delivered Travis' victory or death letter. The Alamo was on their minds as they set to work creating the new, permanent Texas government.

Washington-on-the-Brazos was a tiny ferry crossing on the Brazos River. There were few cabins and buildings. The convention members met in a gunsmith shop that was under construction. They tried to stay dry in the cold, pouring rain that had turned the town into a muddy mess.

Duwali or Diwal'li (c. 1756–1839) was the main chief of the Cherokee and associated tribes in the eastern part of the Republic of Texas in the 1830s. English-speaking people called the Cherokee leader Chief Bowles (or Bowl), Bold Hunter, or the Bowl. His father was Scottish, and his mother was Cherokee. Houston and Duwali had a good relationship, but Mirabeau Lamar—the Texas Republic president after Houston—distrusted the Cherokee and ordered the chief and his people to leave Texas. The Texas militia killed Duwali, who was carrying a sword given to him by Houston, at the Battle of the Neches River in 1839.

On March 2, 1836, the delegates signed a declaration of independence. Sam Houston's signature looked like "I am Houston" sprawled across the document with a flourish. A second letter arrived from Travis on March 6, informing the government that he and his men were running out of ammunition and couldn't hold out much longer.

The Texan defenders of the Alamo, including Davy Crockett holding a rifle above his head, battle the Mexicans.

Houston left the convention to take charge of the military in the field.

The rest of the delegates worked on drafting a constitution for the new country of Texas. The document they wrote was similar to the Constitution of the United States. There would be a legislative body made up of a House of Representatives and a Senate. A president and vice president would lead the executive branch. A Supreme Court would head up the judiciary branch, and lower courts would be created as needed. Unlike the U.S. Constitution, however, the Texas document formally legalized slavery. David G. Burnet was named the temporary president until formal elections could be held.

The siege of the Alamo began on February 23, 1836. The Texan army battled the Mexican troops for 13 days. On March 6, the Mexicans stormed the fort and wiped out its defenders.

Word reached the convention that the Alamo had fallen to Santa Anna. The defenders were dead, and Texans were fleeing the countryside. The government leaders left Washington-on-the-Brazos, heading toward Harrisburg, then Galveston Island. Houston had been scrambling to reach the Alamo when he heard the news. He retreated toward Fannin. ॐ

6 VICTORY

⸙ↂ⸙

Mexican General José de Urrea found Colonel Fannin, his men, and the stubborn oxen at La Bahia in Goliad. Fannin took one look at the Mexican army marching across the flat plains and realized that he would be fighting a losing battle. He surrendered to Urrea with the understanding that they would be treated as prisoners of war. For a while, they were. Urrea sent a message to Santa Anna, and the Mexicans and their prisoners waited for his response. When it came, even Urrea didn't like what he heard.

Santa Anna ordered his general to execute Fannin and most of his men. The Mexican leader said they weren't prisoners of war, they were pirates. Gathering up the Texans, Urrea's officers

Antonio Lopez de Santa Anna led the Mexican army in its fight against the Texans.

told them they were being moved. Instead, they broke them into smaller groups, marched them outside, and shot them. Fannin was shot on the grounds of La Bahia.

The deaths at the Alamo and Goliad infuriated the men marching with Houston. They clamored to attack the Mexican forces. But Houston knew that with about 1,000 men, he had no chance of defeating Santa Anna and the nearly 5,000 soldiers he had gathered. Houston ordered a retreat.

Some of Houston's men left the ranks to join their families as they fled Texas for the

Artist Lewis A. Collas created this portrait of Sam Houston in about 1836.

safety of the United States. Others left because they couldn't stand the idea of retreating from Santa Anna and didn't respect Houston's decisions. They believed that Houston had them running away like chickens.

By the time Houston neared the Brazos River in April, the Mexican forces had split into prongs. Santa Anna and his men swept toward Harrisburg, Texas, to wait for the arrival of another Mexican general.

The Texans were tired of retreating. Every day, they urged Houston to stand and fight. The temporary government sent messages for the general to attack Santa Anna, but Houston continued to march his men away from the Mexican forces—until they came to a fork in a wagon road. One way went toward Harrisburg and Buffalo Bayou. The other road led to Louisiana and American soldiers. Houston took the Harrisburg road. By this time, Houston and his men had two cannons they called the twin sisters. The cannons were gifts from the state of Ohio.

Santa Anna moved down the west side of the San Jacinto River, crossing a bridge at Vince's Bayou. The swampy land was full of water after days of rain. The surrounding area was a mix of grassy meadows, marshes, and sheltering woods. The nearest way out for miles was back over Vince's Bridge.

Houston stopped not far from the bridge and set up camp behind a line of trees. Less than a mile away, Santa Anna camped on a low hill. His army threw up a barricade of luggage and equipment and waited for reinforcements to arrive under the leadership of General Martin Perfecto de Cos. When de Cos crossed Vince's Bridge, Santa Anna's forces grew by nearly 1,400 men.

At the Texan camp, the men pleaded with Houston to attack Santa Anna, but Houston

This 6-pound (2.7-kilogram) smoothbore gun is just one kind of weapon that was used in the Mexican War.

refused. He knew that the timing had to be just right. On the morning of April 21, after a sound night's sleep, Houston met with his generals. His restless troops had intercepted a barge with sup-

plies for the Mexican army. They used flour to make dough patties and slaughtered cattle for a hearty breakfast.

Leaving about 200 men at camp, Houston began to move more than 700 of his men along a forested ridge. Towering oak, arching magnolias, and dense evergreen trees hid their movements from Santa Anna. Wagons and men pulled the "twin sisters" into place.

Houston sent his scout "Deaf" Smith with some other men to Vince's Bridge. They burned it down to ensure that no more Mexican troops could reach Santa Anna and that Santa Anna would not be able to escape easily. Unfortunately, it also meant that Houston and his men had no immediate way to retreat, but they were willing to take their chances.

After days of waiting, Santa Anna decided that Houston would never muster the courage to attack him. The Mexican encampment settled into an afternoon siesta. It was the moment Houston had been waiting for, and he finally ordered his men to attack.

The Texans moved forward firing rifles and cannons into the Mexican barricade. Deaf Smith rode up, shouting that the bridge was down and Houston, astride a large white stallion, galloped across the front of the line. His officers and men

Deaf Smith County, Texas, is named after Sam Houston's favorite Texas revolution scout, Captain Erastus "Deaf" Smith. He was hearing impaired, but that didn't stop him from being an excellent scout for Houston and his troops. As a scout, Smith secretly tracked enemy troops and determined their strength and location so he could report to Houston. After leading a group of men to destroy Vince's Bridge, Smith is said to have charged back and forth across the battlefield at the start of the Battle at San Jacinto to let the Texans know, "The bridge is down. They can't get away. Victory or death!"

fanned across the plain.

At last, the frustrated Texans swept over the Mexican barricade. They screeched "Remember the Alamo!" "Remember La Bahia!" or "Remember Goliad!" Startled Mexican troops dashed around the encampment, stumbling over the bodies of those who had already been killed. The Texans used their guns to shoot or club the Mexican troops. Others pulled out knives and hatchets and stabbed their opponents to death.

Santa Anna rode a horse away from the battlefield. He would later say, "So sudden and fierce was the enemy's charge that the earth seemed to move and tremble." Many Mexican officers were killed instantly. The rest of the troops ran in every direction, trying to avoid the wrath of the Texans and the fire of the twin sisters.

A bullet shattered Houston's left ankle about the same time his horse was shot out from under him. With his boot filling with blood, he climbed

The Texans fought fiercely at the Battle of San Jacinto to avenge the deaths of their comrades at the Alamo and La Bahia.

on a horse and continued to lead his troops. The initial battle lasted less than 20 minutes, but Texans cornered and killed Mexican troops well into the evening. Houston tried to call his men to order and get them to regroup, but they were too fired up to listen. As twilight fell, the agonizing screams of the Mexican soldiers pierced the night. Wolves skulked across the meadow and bayou to feast on the bodies.

The Texans killed an astonishing 630 Mexican soldiers and captured another 730. Only eight Texans were killed and about 30 wounded. Houston

For more than 100 years, artists and most historians have said that Sam Houston shattered his right ankle during the Battle of San Jacinto. The huge memorial statue to him just south of Huntsville, Texas, shows him with a cane in his right hand. A famous painting in the Texas state Capitol shows Houston resting against an oak, his right leg injured. However, in a letter he wrote to his wife, Margaret, in 1853, Houston talks about the San Jacinto injury to his left leg. His son Andrew Jackson Houston wrote in a 1938 book, "The general's left ankle was shattered by a copper ball." The Sam Houston Memorial Museum shows a wounded left leg in its exhibits to reflect Houston's letter and his son's book.

wrote in his official report that "every officer and man proved himself worthy of the cause in which he battled."

The day after his stunning win at San Jacinto, Houston was resting under a tree on the field. He wrote letters to two people: President Andrew Jackson and a young sweetheart named Anna. Houston braided leaves into a garland and sent them with a playful note to Anna saying they were his laurels of victory. (Anna eventually married the man who delivered Houston's messages.)

Toward the end of the day, some of Houston's men approached the camp with Santa Anna in tow. The muddy man they had captured was confirmed as *El Presidente* by the Mexican leader's already-captured secretary and one of his generals. Santa Anna sat on a crate next to the mat on which Houston was sprawled, nursing his mangled ankle.

The Mexican leader asked

Houston to be gracious in victory. Texans crowded around the two men. Most want to kill Santa Anna on the spot. Houston asked Santa Anna why on earth he should be merciful when Santa Anna had slaughtered Travis, Fannin, and their men. Why should he spare the man's life when he had denied the Texan soldiers a decent burial and instead burned their bodies? Because of this, the Texans

The captive Santa Anna (standing left between the men with guns) is brought to Sam Houston (sitting against the tree).

hadn't even bothered to burn the Mexican casualties at San Jacinto; their bodies were left to rot on the field or be devoured by wolves.

Santa Anna spoke in Spanish. One of his generals translated. Surely Houston must understand that the Texans were not prisoners of war, but pirates acting against the orders of Mexico. Houston didn't care about Santa Anna's excuses, but he did have a reason for keeping the man alive: so he could return to Mexico and endorse lasting independence for Texas. The two men worked out a treaty. Mexican troops would move south of the Rio Grande, and Mexico would recognize Texas as an independent republic, or country.

Texas' President Burnet and other officials traveled to San Jacinto as soon as they heard about the victory. When they arrived, Santa Anna signed two treaties, one public and the other private. The public treaty ordered the release of Texan and Mexican prisoners. Property was to be restored to Texan owners. Mexican troops would retreat beyond the Rio Grande. The terms of the private treaty provided for Santa Anna to be released. In exchange for his life, Santa Anna agreed to negotiate a permanent treaty with Mexico that formally recognized Texas as an independent country and established the Rio Grande as its southern boundary.

As grand as all this sounded, it wasn't going to

happen. Before Santa Anna could leave Texas on the ship *Invincible*, the Mexican government denounced him and any treaties. Santa Anna was toppled from power, and Mexico would continue to fight. Santa Anna eventually made his way back to Mexico. He came into power again, only to die destitute and relatively unknown.

Burnet, meanwhile, struggled with officers who didn't like taking orders. Some defied the government and threatened to impose military rule. Comanche and Caddo tribes attacked a fort on the Navasota River. There was no money and there were not enough men for the government to defend the fort or retaliate against the Indians.

Burnet faced an empty treasury, and even the United States was slow to lend the new country money. Texas had very few roads and no regular mail. Many people who returned to their homes found them gone, their property destroyed. Suddenly, they were struggling to survive. Burnet was overwhelmed.

The Mexican presidency changed hands 36 times between 1833 and 1855. Santa Anna took control of the country 11 different times, beginning with his first nomination in 1833. Although he was elected president, he soon began ruling as a dictator. His defeat at San Jacinto resulted in his loss of power, but an impressive victory against a French invasion at Vera Cruz helped build renewed support for the general. He ruled again from 1841 until 1844, when the country revolted against him. In 1853, he became Mexico's leader once again, only to be forced to leave the country two years later.

The San Jacinto Monument in Harris County, Texas, is the world's tallest monument tower.

Burnet set a date in September for Texans to elect their permanent officials. At that time, voters would be asked to approve the constitution, and elect a president, senators, and members of the House of Representatives. They would also be asked to express their views on annexation to the United States.

While Burnet planned the election and struggled with the problems of the new republic, Houston struggled with problems of his own. His injured ankle was badly in need of treatment. He got on a ship at Galveston Island and sailed to New Orleans. 🍂

7 MR. PRESIDENT

ⵦⵦⵦ

Sam Houston went to New Orleans to find a good doctor. His ankle was infected, and there were still bone fragments in the wound. He fainted on the dock as he stepped off the ship. The same doctor who worked on Houston's shoulder after the Battle of Horseshoe Bend worked on his ankle. Houston was near death at times, but he slowly recovered. As a result of his San Jacinto injury, Houston limped and suffered from pain off and on for the rest of his life.

Back in Texas, two men were in the race for president. One was Stephen F. Austin, who had led the first Anglo settlers into Texas. The other candidate was Henry Smith, who was governor of Texas under the provisional government. Houston returned to

Sam Houston was elected the first president of the Republic of Texas in 1836.

Texas and, just 11 days before the election, became the third candidate. The election was held on September 5, 1836, and Houston won by a landslide. Mirabeau Lamar, another San Jacinto hero, was elected vice president. Texas citizens also voted to accept the constitution and to seek annexation to the United States.

When the Republic of Texas was formed, boundaries with Mexico and the United States had to be determined. The Texans and the Mexicans both claimed a large portion of land to the west of the Republic.

The first Texas Congress, made up of 14 senators and 29 representatives, met in Columbia, Texas, on October 3, 1836. Burnet, still serving as interim president, urged land grants to veterans and

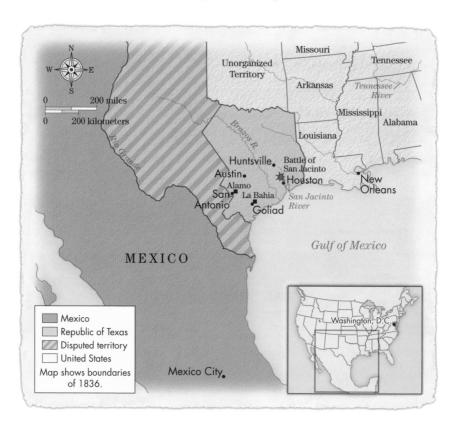

reminded the citizens of Texas that the republic was already in debt for more than $1.2 million. Houston took the oath of office as president of the Texas Republic on October 22: "I, Sam Houston, President of the Republic of Texas, do solemnly and sincerely swear, that I will faithfully execute the duties of my office, and to the best of my ability, preserve, protect, and defend the Constitution of the Republic."

In his inaugural address, Houston called for peace treaties with the Indians and vigilance regarding the Mexicans. He wanted Texas annexed to the United States. He asked the Senate to confirm his appointments to the new cabinet, including the appointment of Stephen F. Austin as secretary of state. Austin, likely weakened by his imprisonment in Mexico, died a little more than two months later.

Stephen Austin died December 27, 1836, shortly after Sam Houston appointed him secretary of state.

One of the first orders of business for the new government was selecting a capital city. Two brothers who were promoting the new city of Houston offered buildings and housing to the government, so Houston was chosen as a temporary capital.

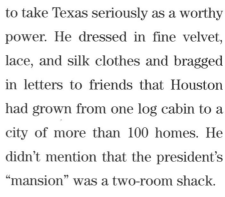

Sam Houston wanted the world to take Texas seriously as a worthy power. He dressed in fine velvet, lace, and silk clothes and bragged in letters to friends that Houston had grown from one log cabin to a city of more than 100 homes. He didn't mention that the president's "mansion" was a two-room shack.

In the meantime, the Texas Congress set the boundaries for Texas, even though Mexico refused to recognize the republic's independence. The eastern border with the state of Louisiana was worked out with surveyors from the U.S. government. The Texas Congress formed 23 counties. Houston and the Texas Congress worked to establish a judicial system and local public safety offices in each county. Mail delivery was also set up.

On Texas' western frontier, Houston worried about Indian tribes being treated fairly and about raids by the Mexican military. The Texas Congress initially passed acts to station soldiers in forts and trading posts. Houston eventually disbanded the formal military. He relied on local militias, rangers, and troops called up for special duty.

Houston turned his attention to his Cherokee friends and submitted the Cherokee land treaty he had negotiated just before the war to the Texas Congress for approval. But the Senate killed the treaty.

During Houston's administration (1836–1838), the public debt soared to more than $3.2 million. Texas did not have enough money to pay its bills. Most Texans, including Houston, worked for annexation to the United States. Almost one year to the day after declaring independence, the U.S. government formally recognized Texas as a country, but did not take action on annexation.

Houston was also dealing with grumblers in his administration. His vice president hated him and worked against Houston's policies. Former president Burnet publicly insulted Houston, only to have Houston call him a hog thief. Burnet challenged Houston to a duel, but Houston ignored him.

During the last months of his administration, Houston was depressed and spent more and more time drinking. The constitution of Texas said that the president could not serve two terms in a row.

The 1830 Indian Removal Act authorized U.S. officials to remove, often forcibly, all tribes east of the Mississippi River and settle them on western lands. In 1838, the government relocated more than 16,000 Cherokee to present-day Oklahoma. The Cherokee traveled grueling routes westward that became known as the Trail of Tears. Thousands of Cherokee died as a result of the Nunahi-Duna-Dlo-Hilu-I, or "trail where they cried." Today, the U.S. National Park Service's Trail of Tears National Historic Trail covers 2,200 miles (3,520 km) through nine states.

*President Sam
Houston enters
the newly
founded city
of Houston.*

Houston didn't want Lamar to become president,
especially since Lamar openly despised the
Cherokee and other tribes. But it looked like Lamar
had a good chance of winning the election.

Two other men entered the presidential race, but one drowned and the other shot himself in the head before the election. It was obvious that Lamar would become the next president of Texas.

Houston spiraled further into depression and drinking. He was in a dark mood but managed to pull himself together.

Houston wasn't invited to Lamar's inauguration, but as the outgoing president, he appeared before the crowd to wave good-bye. The crowd cheered Houston, who was wearing a powdered wig and clothing similar to that worn by George Washington, America's first president. He spoke to the adoring crowd for more than three hours as the furious Lamar sat nearby. By the time the eloquent Houston was done, Lamar was so angry he was speechless. Lamar's secretary had to read the new president's inaugural address. Houston had gotten the last word.

Lamar and the Texas Congress moved the capital to a spot along the Colorado River and called it Austin. Houston didn't want to stick around and watch someone else govern his Texas, least of all Mirabeau Lamar. In 1839, he went to Tennessee to visit Andrew Jackson at the Hermitage. On the way, he stopped at the home of a friend in Alabama who raised horses. His friend's wife was hosting a strawberry festival, and Houston stayed for the party. In the garden, he met his friend's 20-year-old

*Joshua Houston
(1822–1902) was one of
Sam Houston's frequent
companions. A black-
smith and carpenter,
he was also one of
Houston's slaves. The
Houstons taught their
slaves, including
Joshua, how to read
and write. Joshua was
allowed to keep the
money he earned work-
ing for other families.
When Sam Houston
died, Joshua stayed in
Huntsville, Texas, and
became a city alderman
and county commis-
sioner. In 1888, he was
a member of the Texas
delegation to the
Republican National
Convention. He is
buried near one of his
wives in Huntsville's
Oakwood Cemetery,
not far from the grave
of his former master.*

sister-in-law, violet-eyed Margaret Lea. Margaret was smitten with the 46-year-old Houston. The feeling was mutual.

Houston left Margaret with a bouquet of flowers. When he returned a few months later, he learned that Margaret's religious family was dead-set against her relationship with Houston. He was too old and a drinker, and he did not go to church. Margaret said she would change all that and vowed to marry Houston. They planned a spring 1840 wedding, and Houston headed back to Texas. What he found infuriated him.

While Houston was falling in love, Lamar was raising troops to fight the Cherokee and other tribes. Mexico had recognized the Cherokee land boundaries, and Houston had hoped his Texas land treaty would pass one day. Lamar had other ideas. His government made such strict demands on the Cherokee that the aging Chief Bowles and his warriors balked and wanted to fight. The chief and his warriors fought a company of Texans and lost. As the chief was leaving the battlefield with his injured horse, he was shot in the back. He struggled to sit up and face the Texas troops. The captain of the attacking company placed his pistol against Chief Bowles's temple and fired.

Houston was livid when he heard the news. He claimed the chief was a much better man than his murderers. Energized by the fights with the tribes, Lamar sent an expedition to Santa Fe, New Mexico, to wrest it from the hands of Mexico. Every man in the expedition was captured by the Mexican forces.

Mirabeau Buonaparte Lamar was born in Georgia in 1798. He served the Republic of Texas as vice president under Sam Houston, and later as president.

In May 1840, Houston and Margaret married in Marion, Alabama. The newlyweds settled in Texas at Cedar Point on Galveston Bay. Houston's friends predicted the marriage wouldn't last a year. 🕮

Chapter

8 FAMILY MAN AND AMERICAN

❧❦❧

Sam Houston ran for president of Texas again in 1841 and was elected. The government debt was even larger than during his first term. He couldn't even afford to buy firewood for the president's home. To make matters worse, looters had ransacked the home after Lamar packed up and left the doors open. Houston had to start from scratch. In his earlier days, he might have started drinking as a way to cope with these problems. But his wife, Margaret, had convinced him to stop drinking. She knew that was a great accomplishment and decided that her dream of getting her husband to go to church could wait.

Houston cut the country's budget and reduced the payroll. Santa Anna, back in power in Mexico,

The city of Houston, Texas, was established in 1836.

was not happy about Lamar's Santa Fe raid and threatened to invade Texas. Texans wanted a war, too, after learning the Santa Fe prisoners had been tortured on the way back to Mexico. Houston rallied an army and kept the Mexican forces at bay. He tried to calm the Texans who wanted war. Texas couldn't afford to fight.

Sam Houston moved the government back to the city of Houston, but the people of Austin refused to surrender any of the government records.

Washington-on-the-Brazos saw significant growth during its days as capital. It thrived as the center for cotton trade on the Brazos River. But when the railroads bypassed the town in the 1850s, it began to suffer. Today, the town's former site is home to the Washington-on-the-Brazos State Historical Park and the Star of the Republic Museum, which honors Texas heroes.

Washington-on-the-Brazos became the compromise capital. When those in Austin still refused to hand over the government's records, Houston gave up and worked without them.

Washington-on-the-Brazos was a little larger than Austin, but it was still not capital material. The war department was housed in a log cabin. The Senate met above a grocery store, and the House of Representatives met above a saloon. Often, House members never made it past the saloon and into the session, so Houston built steps on the outside of the building so the men could bypass the bar.

Houston started drinking again. He had sent Margaret to live near her family when Santa Anna had threatened invasion. Now he asked her to come live with him in Washington-on-the-Brazos so that she could help him stay sober. Soon their first child, Sam Jr., was born. The Houstons eventually had eight children.

Texas sold property and received money from U.S. well-wishers. Houston strengthened a settlement

The city of Austin was established in 1840 and served as the capital of the Republic of Texas. Today, it is the capital of the state of Texas.

program that encouraged settlers to come to Texas. He sought peace treaties with the Indians, encouraged trade along the southern and western borders, and worked to end a civil war among three Texas counties. He even negotiated a temporary truce with Santa Anna.

Working for annexation to the United States was at the top of Houston's list of priorities. It was no small task. When Houston left office in 1844, the new president, Anson Jones, continued work on the annexation issue. Jones had been Houston's secretary of state and often ran the government toward the end of Houston's term. Houston was absent a lot, taking time off to care for Margaret, who was depressed and suffered from asthma. Jones grew to dislike Houston during this time and often wrote snide comments on letters from him.

Anson Jones served as Sam Houston's secretary of state. He was elected president of Texas in 1844.

Things got confusing when England and France both began trying to reinstitute ties with Texas. Mexico warned it would go to war with the United States if Texas were annexed.

Then Houston said that if the United States didn't annex Texas by March 4, 1845, he would change course and fight annexation.

James K. Polk was running for president of the United States. He wanted both Texas and the Oregon Territory to join the country, and he spoke out in favor of U.S. expansion during his campaign. Outgoing President John Tyler urged the U.S. Congress to approve a resolution for the annexation of Texas. The resolution passed. The paperwork was completed in April 1845 and sent to Texas president Jones. The terms of the resolution for annexation had to be accepted by January 1, 1846.

A convention met in Austin on July 4, and the delegates voted in favor of annexation. The attendees drafted a state constitution and submitted both the resolution for annexation and the constitution to the citizens of Texas for a vote. On October 13, annexation was approved by a vote of

General Antonio Lopez de Santa Anna, president of Mexico, and James Gadsden, the U.S. minister to Mexico, signed the Gadsden Purchase in 1853. The treaty formally placed the Mexican border west of El Paso, Texas. The United States paid Mexico $10 million for 29,640 square miles (77,064 square km) of land that would become part of the state of Arizona and the southern part of New Mexico. The land purchase allowed for the development of the southern transcontinental railroad, connecting the western territories with the eastern part of the United States.

4,174 to 312. The U.S. Congress approved the Texas constitution, and President Polk signed the act creating the state of Texas on December 29, 1845. Two months later, in a special ceremony, Texas lowered the Lone Star state flag and raised the U.S. flag above it.

Margaret Lea Houston

Now that Texas was part of the United States, Margaret was hopeful that Houston would settle down with their growing family and finally leave politics behind. She even wrote him a long poem saying how happy she was that he would soon retire. Toward the end of the poem she wrote:

> *Thy task is done. The holy shade*
> *Of calm retirement waits thee now,*
> *The lamp of hope relit hath shed*
> *Its sweet refulgence o'er thy brow.*

Houston barely had time to say he was a retired family man before he was elected one of Texas's senators, along with Thomas Rusk. He was 53 years old when he arrived in Washington, D.C., without

Margaret and the children. She had decided it was better to keep a welcoming home in Texas where Houston could retreat from political battles. The United States was at war with Mexico, a war that began in April 1846 and wouldn't end until February 1848. Historians still argue over which country started the war, but the reason for the war was clear—the annexation of Texas.

Houston wrote to his wife and children weekly. His letters were full of advice to Sam Jr. about being good and reading about Greek heroes. In Washington, D.C., Houston spoke at meetings about the dangers of drink, to help him stay sober. He attended church every Sunday and wrote to Margaret:

Sam Houston Jr. was born at Washington-on-the-Brazos, Texas, on May 25, 1843. After serving in the Confederate Army during the Civil War, he became a physician. He eventually gave up medicine and became an author.

> *Washington, November 18, 1849*
> *Remember, Love, you are to write me once a week when you are able … and nothing on earth can make me more happy than to know that you are happy. That embraces*

all that are dear to me. As it is Sunday night, I will not write to you on any matters of business. My love to all. Ever thine. p.s. Tell Sam, Nannie and Maggy that I have preserved all the roses and chrysanthemums which they gave me. I will keep them. Thine.

Houston, still tall and distinguished, was white-haired by this time. He wore white beaver hats and carried a walking stick. He often threw a brightly colored blanket over his shoulders. This probably annoyed one of his Senate colleagues, his old nemesis John C. Calhoun of South Carolina. Finally, Houston had a chance to be a thorn in his side.

Thomas Jefferson Rusk (1803–1857) served with Sam Houston as one of the first U.S. senators from Texas. Rusk was a lawyer born in South Carolina. He fought at the Battle of San Jacinto and was commander of the Texas army for a short time. Rusk also served as chief justice of the Texas Supreme Court.

Calhoun was a loud proponent of slavery and states' rights. The members of Congress were divided over whether new territory should be slave or free.

Houston owned slaves and Texas was a Southern slave state, but he believed the Union should be preserved at all costs. Calhoun's and Houston's intense disagreement reflected what was going on in the United States between the North and South. Houston told his fellow sena-

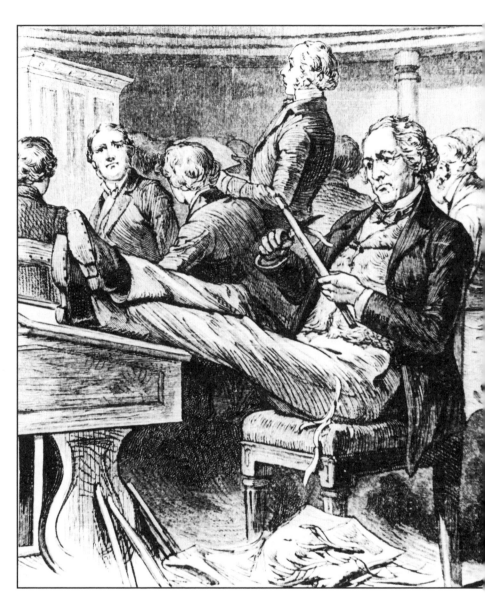

Sam Houston whittles in the U.S. Senate.

tors as early as 1847, "Let not the name of Texas, his home, the last to be incorporated in to the Union, ever be blasphemed by the word 'disunion.' Let not the Union be severed." His stand never wavered.

In 1847, the Houstons had built another home, this one in Huntsville, Texas. The home had a long hall running through the middle of the house.

Sam and Margaret Houston had eight children, four boys and four girls. Temple Lea Houston was the youngest, born in 1860.

On cool spring days, with both doors thrown open at the ends of the hall, a breeze would follow the scurrying kids and dogs up and down the hallway. Houston was a little more at ease and could enjoy his family life a bit more now that the Texas Legislature had approved U.S. Senator Henry Clay's compromise bill in 1850. Clay was known as the Great Compromiser because he helped draft the Missouri Compromise, the Compromise of 1850, and other legislation that delayed the start of the Civil War. His latest compromise, in 1850, helped preserve the balance between the North and the South. ✑

Kentucky Senator Henry Clay fought to keep the states together but died in 1852, nine years before the war between the North and South. Sam Houston was one of the senators who accompanied Clay's body from Washington, D.C., to Kentucky for burial.

Chapter 9

TEXAS LEAVES THE UNION, HOUSTON LEAVES THIS LIFE

❧❧❧

By 1852, Houston and his friends were thinking of a Houston presidency—this time as president of the United States. Houston clubs had begun to spring up all over the country. Although he didn't actively campaign for the presidency, Houston hoped for it. His grassroots approach didn't work, though, because political parties and conventions dominated the political process. When Houston saw how many candidates wanted to run for president in the Democratic Party, he bowed out. Franklin Pierce was elected president, and in the second year of his presidency, the slave issue reared its ugly head yet again.

The new Kansas-Nebraska Act did away with Senator Clay's balancing act. Congress voted to let

In 1856, Sam Houston ran for governor of the state of Texas. He lost the election and returned to Washington, D.C., to complete his term in the U.S. Senate.

new territories decide for themselves whether or not they would be slave states. Houston was afraid that hotheads from both the North and the South would turn Kansas and Nebraska into battle-grounds. He was sure the bill would eventually lead to the downfall of the nation.

When Congress recessed, the restless Houston returned to Texas. He and his family divided their time among three homes, one of them near Margaret's family. While there, he welcomed the birth of their son Andrew Jackson Houston. He worried that he was the only person in the South who wanted to preserve the Union. He also told Margaret he was ready to be baptized.

Franklin Pierce was the 14th president of the United States and served from 1853 to 1857.

In 1856, Senator Houston watched as pro-slavery and pro-abolition forces fought in Kansas. A man named John Brown said God told him to set the slaves free, so he and his followers killed five slavery supporters. Elsewhere, a congressman from South Carolina nearly beat to death a senator from Massachusetts.

Senator Calhoun had died and his successor was Mississippi's Jefferson Davis. He later became president of the Confederacy, the group of 11 Southern states that split from the Northern states. Back in Texas, a Davis man was running for governor. Houston didn't want someone in favor of secession to become governor, so he ran against him.

Houston traveled more than 1,500 miles (2,400 km) by buggy in less than 70 days as he campaigned for governor. He gave nearly 50 speeches, some of them more than four hours long. He dressed in common clothes and kissed plenty of women and babies, but he lost the race and returned to the Senate to finish his term. Though politically weakened by his loss in Texas, he used every opportunity to support the Union and help Indian tribes. At the end of his term, tired of Washington and weary of the political unrest in the North and South, Houston retired to his home in Cedar Point.

In 1859, Houston ran again for governor of Texas. He made only one speech this time, but voters saw that Houston's predictions about the Kansas-Nebraska Act had been right. The South

> *Houston served as one of the U.S. senators from Texas from 1846 to 1859. At the start of his service, it took him about six weeks by carriage and steamboat to travel from Texas to Washington, D.C. By 1859, it only took him about six days. What made the difference? In 1859, Houston could ride a train for part of the journey.*

didn't benefit. Texas didn't benefit. Houston won the election, and Margaret and the children went with him to Austin, which had become the permanent capital of Texas.

The house for the governor's family was small for Sam, Margaret, their children, and the family dogs. Son Andrew was always pulling pranks and even locked the Texas senators in their chambers once. Andrew's shenanigans were probably the only funny thing happening in the Texas Legislature.

Jefferson Davis was a senator from Mississippi and served as secretary of war under President Franklin Pierce. He became the first and only president of the Confederate States of America.

Less than a month after Houston became governor, the South Carolina Legislature circulated a resolution saying that any state had the right to secede from the Union. Houston defended the Union. The Texas governor's philosophy was to let the North be the North and the South be the South.

Houston's even-tempered approach won him some fans in the rest of the country, and he soon found himself running for president of the United States again. He disliked the party convention system and insisted that if he were nominated, it must be by the people. In April 1860, on the San Jacinto battle-field, Houston's supporters nominated him for president. The Republican Party nominated Abraham Lincoln. Houston was sure the South would secede if Lincoln was elected. He accepted his nomination.

There were four men, including Houston, running against Lincoln. Houston feared this would split the votes and allow Lincoln to win. Then, Margaret gave birth to their last child, and it was not an easy birth. Houston did not leave her bedside or even undress for 10 days. He decided to withdraw from the presidential race.

On November 6, the nation elected Abraham Lincoln, and Houston knew the South would secede. Secretly, he hoped he could work out a way for Texas to become a republic again, instead of becoming part of the Confederacy. It didn't happen.

In January 1861, Southern states started leaving the Union.

In 1858, Abraham Lincoln used the famous phrase "A house divided against itself cannot stand" to emphasize that the United States would not survive being divided over the issue of slavery. Eight years before that, Sam Houston said "A nation divided against itself cannot stand," when he supported the Compromise of 1850, a controversial set of congressional bills designed to handle the issue of slavery in the country's new territories and states. Lincoln didn't borrow the phrase from Houston, though. The words are based on a proverb in the Bible and had been used by many people before Lincoln made the words famous.

A crowd of people gathered to watch as Abraham Lincoln was sworn in as president of the United States on March 4, 1861.

Jefferson Davis was elected president of the South's provisional government.

In Texas, a group of men in favor of leaving the Union held a convention in February and voted to secede. Houston was furious. The group had no right to decide what Texas would do. There was a

constitution that guided the government, and it was being trampled. The convention voted to remove Houston from office because he refused to swear an oath of allegiance to the Confederacy. Houston wrote a letter to the people. Part of it said:

> *Fellow citizens, in the name of your rights and liberties, which I believe have been trampled upon, I refuse to take this oath ... In the name of my own conscience and my own manhood ... I refuse to take this oath ... I love Texas too well to bring strife and bloodshed upon her.*

In 1862, the Houstons moved to a home in Huntsville. His battle with the convention lost, Houston finally supported a Confederate Texas. Sam Jr. joined the Confederate forces and was left on a battlefield to die, much like his father at Horseshoe Bend. He was rescued by a chaplain and eventually returned to his family.

Even though he publicly supported Texas and had a son in the Confederate Army, people still attacked Houston and called him names. He could ignore the attacks, but sitting on the sidelines during a war made him restless. He kept himself occupied by making out his will and leaving instructions on how his children should live, what they should read, and how they should behave.

After Houston's death, his widow, Margaret Moffette Lea, and their children moved from Huntsville to Independence, Texas, to be closer to her family. In 1867, Margaret and the youngest children were preparing to visit married daughter Nannie for the Christmas holidays. Before they left, however, Margaret died unexpectedly of yellow fever, a deadly virus that was sweeping the community. Her body was quickly buried in a deep grave near her mother's tomb in an attempt to help stop the spread of the disease. Two of her daughters, a family friend, and a servant laid the body of the deeply religious Margaret to rest after a neighboring preacher refused to come to the grave.

In poor health, 70-year-old Houston spent nearly a month at a resort. With his health somewhat improved, when he returned home he began to take daily walks to the nearby prison, where he talked to the Northern prisoners. When he wasn't out walking, he often sat in a rocking chair under the shade of a tree in his yard.

In July 1863, word came that the South's General Robert E. Lee had been defeated at the Battle of Gettysburg and that the North's General Ulysses S. Grant defeated the Southern forces at the Battle of Vicksburg. Soon after these events, Houston returned from a walk to the prison weak and chilled. Margaret put him to bed, where friends visited him and servants fanned him. He developed pneumonia and died on July 26, 1863. Union prisoners built his coffin, and he was buried in Huntsville's Oakwood Cemetery.

Sam Houston's life was long and colorful. From bored young

farm boy to governor of the state of Texas, he remained true to his dreams. From the time he set foot on its soil, he put all his effort into doing what he thought was best for Texas as a territory, a republic, and a U.S. state. His beloved Texas was always on his mind. On his deathbed, with Margaret reading the Bible at his side, Houston whispered "Texas. Texas. Margaret," and drew his last breath. 🙰

HOUSTON'S LIFE

1793

Born on March 2
in Rockbridge
County, Virginia

1806

His father dies
unexpectedly

1807

Moves to
Tennessee with
his mother and
siblings

1800

1799

The Rosetta stone,
which was the key to
understanding Egyptian
hieroglyphics, is found
near Rosetta, Egypt

1805

General anesthesia
is first used in
surgery

WORLD EVENTS

1809

Runs away to live with a band of Cherokee on the Tennessee River

1810

Is adopted as a son by Cherokee Chief Oolooteka

1814

Seriously wounded at the Battle of Horseshoe Bend in the War of 1812

1810

1809

Louis Braille of France, inventor of a writing system for the blind, is born

1810

Bernardo O'Higgins leads Chile in its fight for independence from Spain

HOUSTON'S LIFE

1827

Becomes governor
of Tennessee

1829

Resigns as
governor and
reunites with
Oolooteka and
the Cherokee

1825

1823

Mexico becomes
a republic

1827

Modern-day
matches are
invented by
coating the end
of a wooden
stick with
phosphorus

1829

The first practical
sewing machine is
invented by French
tailor Barthélemy
Thimonnier

WORLD EVENTS

1831

Mother,
Elizabeth, dies

1835

Becomes a
major general in
the Texas army

1836

Defeats and captures
Santa Anna at San
Jacinto; elected
president of the
Republic of Texas

1835

1833

Great Britain
abolishes slavery

HOUSTON'S LIFE

1841

Begins his
second term
as president of
the Republic
of Texas

1846

Becomes one of
Texas's first
U.S. senators

1840

1840

Auguste Rodin,
famous sculptor of
The Thinker, is born

1846

Irish potato
famine reaches
its worst

WORLD EVENTS

1861

Refuses to take an oath of allegiance to the Confederacy and is removed as governor

1863

Dies of pneumonia in Huntsville, Texas, on July 26

1859

Ends his last term as U.S. senator and is elected governor of Texas

1860

1862

Victor Hugo publishes *Les Misérables*

1858

English scientist Charles Darwin presents his theory of evolution

DATE OF BIRTH: March 2, 1793

BIRTHPLACE: Rockbridge County, Virginia

FATHER: Samuel Houston (1745–1806)

MOTHER: Elizabeth Paxton Houston (1765–1831)

EDUCATION: Little formal education

SPOUSES:: Eliza Allen (married 1829)
Tiana "Diana" Rogers (married 1830–1832)
Margaret Moffette Lea (1819–1867; married May 9, 1840)

CHILDREN: Sam Houston Jr. (1843–1894)
Nancy Elizabeth Houston (1846–1920)
Margaret Lea Houston (1848–1906)
Mary William Houston (1850–1931)
Antoinette Power Houston (1852–1932)
Andrew Jackson Houston (1854–1941)
William Rogers Houston (1858–?)
Temple Lea Houston (1860–1905)

DATE OF DEATH: July 26, 1863

PLACE OF BURIAL: Oakwood Cemetery, Huntsville, Texas

In the Library

Alter, Judy. *Sam Houston Is My Hero.* Fort Worth, Texas: TCU Press, 2003.

Bankston, John. *Antonio Lopez de Santa Anna.* Bear, Del.: Mitchell Lane Publishers, 2004.

Caravantes, Peggy. *An American in Texas: The Story of Sam Houston.* Greensboro, N.C.: Morgan Reynolds Publishing, 2004.

Collier, Christopher, and James Lincoln Collier. *Hispanic America, Texas, and the Mexican War 1835–1850.* Tarrytown, N.Y.: Benchmark Books, 1999.

Nelson, Sheila. *A Proud and Isolated Nation: Americans Take a Stand in Texas.* Philadelphia: Mason Crest Publishers, 2005.

Look for more Signature Lives
books about this era:

James Beckwourth: *Mountaineer, Scout, and Pioneer*

Geronimo: *Apache Warrior*

Crazy Horse: *Sioux Warrior*

Bridget "Biddy" Mason: *From Slave to Businesswoman*

Zebulon Pike: *Explorer and Soldier*

Sarah Winnemucca: *Scout, Activist, and Teacher*

ON THE WEB

For more information on *Sam Houston*, use FactHound to track
down Web sites related to this book.

1. Go to *www.facthound.com*
2. Type in a search word related to this book or this book ID: 075651004X
3. Click on the *Fetch It* button.

FactHound will find the best Web sites for you.

HISTORIC SITES

Sam Houston Memorial Museum
Sam Houston State University
1402 19th St.
Huntsville, TX 77341
936/294-1832
To learn more about the life and times of Sam Houston

San Jacinto Monument and Museum of History
San Jacinto Battleground Historical Park
One Monument Circle
LaPorte, TX 77571-9585
281/479-2421
To see the San Jacinto Monument and learn more about the history of Texas

barge
a large, flat-bottomed boat used for moving goods on rivers and other inland waterways

bludgeon
a weapon, such as a stick

destitute
living in extreme poverty

diplomacy
handling negotiations between people or countries without creating bad feelings

eloquent
expressive and forceful

epic
impressive or heroic

inaugural
related to an inauguration or a beginning

lacrosse
a game in which players use a long-handled stick with a mesh pouch to catch and throw a ball in an attempt to score goals

laurels
crowns made from the branches of the evergreen shrub known as the laurel, which are given to someone to honor an accomplishment

litter
a stretcher

medicine spirit
a guiding spirit that takes the form of an animal

militia
a group of citizens ready to fight when called

nemesis
a dreaded opponent

persistent
standing firm in spite of opposition or difficulties

provisional
temporary

ranks
soldiers

skirmish
to engage in a minor battle

tyranny
power that oppresses people

voracious
extremely eager

whittled
cut small pieces off a chunk of
wood with a knife

Chapter 2

Page 18, line 16: Marshall De Bruhl. *Sword of San Jacinto: A Life of Sam Houston.* New York: Random House, 1993, p.31.

Page 21, line 1: James L. Haley, *Sam Houston.* Norman: University of Oklahoma Press, 2002, page 12.

Chapter 3

Page 30, line 3: Donald Day and Harry Herbert Ullom, ed., *The Autobiography of Sam Houston.* Norman: University of Oklahoma Press, 1954, page 42.

Chapter 4

Page 36, line 3: John Hoyt Williams, *Sam Houston: A Biography of the Father of Texas.* New York: Simon & Schuster, p. 93.

Chapter 5

Page 46, line 5: *Biography Resource Center.* Farmington Hills, Mich.: Thomson Gale, 2004, *http://galenet.galegroup.com/servlet/BioRC.*

Chapter 6

Page 56, line 4: Texas State Library & Archives Commission. "The Battle of San Jacinto," *http://www.tsl.state.tx.s/treasures/republic/san-jacinto.html*

Page 56, line 17: Texas Military Forces Museum. "San Jacinto," *http://www.kwanah.com/txmilus/tnghist5.htm*

Page 58, line 2: Texas State Library & Archives Commission. "Sam Houston's Copy of His Official Report of the Battle of San Jacinto," *http://www.tsl.state.tx.us/treasures/republic/san-jacinto/report-05.html*

Chapter 7

Page 67, line 4: *Sam Houston,* p. 191.

Chapter 8

Page 80, line 21: *Sword of San Jacinto: A Life of Sam Houston,* p. 310.

Page 81, line 24: *The Autobiography of Sam Houston,* p. 223.

Page 83, line 2: Randolph B. Campbell. *Gone to Texas: A History of the Lone Star State.* New York: Oxford University Press, 2003, p. 233.

Chapter 9

Page 93, line 6: James Marquis. *The Raven: A Biography of Sam Houston.* Indianapolis, Ind.: Bobb-Merrill, 1929, p. 412.

Page 95, line 7: *Sword of San Jacinto: A Life of Sam Houston,* p. 402.

Campbell, Randolph B. *Gone to Texas: A History of the Lone Star State*. New York: Oxford University Press, 2003.

Day, Donald, and Harry Herbert Ullom, ed. *The Autobiography of Sam Houston*. Norman: University of Oklahoma Press, 1954.

De Bruhl, Marshall. *Sword of San Jacinto: A Life of Sam Houston*. New York: Random House, 1993.

Haley, James L. *Sam Houston*. Norman: University of Oklahoma Press, 2002.

Marquis, James. *The Raven: A Biography of Sam Houston*. Indianapolis, Ind.: Bobb-Merrill, 1929.

Williams, John Hoyt. *Sam Houston: A Biography of the Father of Texas*. New York: Simon & Schuster, 1993.

Library of Congress
America's Story from America's Library
Jump Back in Time
http://www.americaslibrary.gov/cgi-bin/page.cgi/jb/reform
Western Expansion and Reform 1829–1859

Sam Houston Memorial Museum
Sam Houston State University
Sam Houston: Biographical Perspectives
www.shsu.edu/~pin_www/samhouston/index.html

Santa Anna, Antonio Lopez de, 11,
    12-13, 39, 41, 42, 44-45, 49, 51,
    52, 53, 55, 56, 58-61, 75-76,
    77, 78, 79
Santa Fe, New Mexico, 73, 76
Siege of Bexar, 42
settlers, 9, 20, 25, 37, 39, 65, 78
slavery, 13, 38, 39, 41, 48, 82, 87,
    88, 91
Smith, Erastus "Deaf," 55, 56
Smith, Henry, 65
South Carolina, 37, 82, 89, 90
Stanbery, William, 35-37
Star of the Republic Museum, 76
statehood, 13, 38, 79-80
states' rights, 82

Tahlhontusky (chief), 26
Tejanos, 10
Tennessee, 11, 13, 16, 19, 25, 26, 27,
    28, 29, 31, 33, 34, 35, 71
Texas
    annexation of, 63, 66, 67, 69,
        78-80, 81
    borders of, 39, 68, 78
    capital of, 67, 71, 76
    Cherokee land treaty, 68-69, 72
    Congress of, 66, 68, 69, 71
    constitution of, 11, 46, 48, 62,
        67, 69, 92
    debt of, 67, 69, 75
    elections in, 48, 62-63, 65-66,
        70-71, 79
    flag of, 67, 80
    House of Representatives, 48,
        63, 76

independence from Mexico, 9-10,
    13, 38-39, 42-42, 46, 60
invasion of, 41-42, 44
judicial branch, 48, 68
purchase of, 37, 79
secession of, 92
Senate, 48, 63, 67, 69, 76
state constitution, 11, 46, 48, 79,
    80, 93
statehood of, 13, 38-39, 67, 79-80
Tiana (wife), 34, 37
Trail of Tears, 69
Trail of Tears National Historic Trail,
    69
transcontinental railroad, 79
Travis, William B., 44, 45-46, 47, 59
"twin sisters" (cannons), 53, 55, 56
Tyler, John, 79

Urrea, José de, 11, 51-52
Utah, 44

Vera Cruz, 61
Vince's Bayou, 53
Vince's Bridge, 53, 55, 56

War of 1812, 20, 23-24
Washington, George, 15, 71
Washington-on-the-Brazos, 46, 49,
    76, 77
Washington-on-the-Brazos State
    Historical Park, 76
Weatherford, William. *See* Red Eagle.
Wyoming, 44

yellow fever, 94

Susan R. Gregson has been writing for more than 22 years. She is the author of nearly 20 children's books. She also writes magazine and Internet articles, speeches, and technical reports. Her favorite part of writing books is the research. Sue lives in Minnesota with her husband, two young sons, a dog, nine fish, and the occasional toad in the sock drawer.

Image Credits